Weedy
Sea Dragons,
Spitting Cobras,
and
Other Wild
and Amazing
Animals

By Robyn O'Sullivan

NATIONAL GEOGRAPHIC

WASHINGTON D.C.

One of the world's largest nonprofit scientific and educational organizations, the National Geographic Society was founded in 1888 "for the increase and diffusion of geographic knowledge." Fulfilling this mission, the Society educates and inspires millions every day through its magazines, books, television programs, videos, maps and atlases, research grants, the National Geographic Bee, teacher workshops, and innovative classroom materials. The Society is supported through membership dues, charitable gifts, and income from the sale of its educational products. This support is vital to National Geographic's mission to increase global understanding and promote conservation of our planet through exploration, research, and education.

For more information, please call
1-800-NGS-LINE (647-5463) or write to the following address:
National Geographic Society
1145 17th Street N.W.
Washington, D.C. 20036-4688
U.S.A.

For information about special discounts for bulk purchases, please contact
National Geographic Books Special Sales at ngspecsales@ngs.org

Visit the Society's Web site: www.nationalgeographic.com

Library of Congress Cataloging-in-Publication Data

O'Sullivan, Robyn.
  Weedy sea dragons, spitting cobras, and other wild and amazing animals / by Robyn O'Sullivan.
    p. cm. -- (National Geographic science chapters)
  Includes bibliographical references and index.
  ISBN-13: 978-0-7922-5941-1 (library binding)
  ISBN-10: 0-7922-5941-6 (library binding)
  1. Animal defenses. I. Title. II. Series.
  QL759.O88 2006
  591.47--dc22

                                    2006016337

Photo Credits
Front Cover: © Marian Bacon/Animals Animals; Spine: © National Geographic Image Collection; Endpaper: © National Geographic Image Collection; 2-3: © Roy Toft/ National Geographic Image Collection; 6: © Doug Wechsler; 8: © Chris Johns National Geographic Image Collection; 9: © Getty Images; 10-11: © National Geographic Image Collection; 12-13: © APL/ Corbis; 14: © Bates Littlehales/ National Geographic Image Collection; 15: © Nature Picture Library; 16-17, 18-19 (both): © National Geographic Image Collection; 20: © Joel Sartore/ National Geographic Image Collection; 21: © Animals Animals; 22-23: © APL/ Corbis; 23 (top): © Stuart Westmorland/ The Image Bank/ Getty Images; 23 (bottom): © Gary Bell/ zefa/ Corbis; 24: © Animals Animals; 25: © Getty Images; 26: © Auscape; 27: © Nature Picture Library; 28: © Getty Images; 29: © Auscape; 30: © Nigel Blake; 31: © Nature Picture Library; 32: © Joseph Van Os/ The Image Bank/ Getty Images; 33: © Auscape; 34: © National Geographic Image Collection; 35: © David Fleetham/ Alamy.

Contents

A spiny devil katydid uses its spiny legs to defend itself from much larger animals.

Strange Animals

What in the world is this creature? It's a South American spiny devil katydid. It has spines all over its body. The spines scare off predators that want to eat the katydid.

Not all animals have spines, but all animals do have unique characteristics or behaviors that help them survive. For example, some animals have unusual ways of catching their dinners. Other animals have specialized physical features that keep them safe from predators. Some of these behaviors and characteristics can be pretty strange. Let's take a look at some of the odder animals in the animal kingdom.

If a chameleon gets cold,
it can change to a darker
color that will absorb more
of the sun's warmth.

Chapter 1

What Is Hiding Here?

Some animals hide from predators by blending in with their surroundings. This is called camouflage. An animal's coloring, markings, and body shape can be its camouflage.

Chameleons live in Africa and India. These reptiles can change the color of their skin. It helps them regulate their body temperature. Changing color also makes them difficult to see.

A chameleon can change color in as little as 20 seconds.

9

Weedy Sea Dragons

Can you see an animal in this picture? It's a weedy sea dragon swimming in the seaweed on the ocean floor. A close relative to seahorses, weedy sea dragons live in the warm waters along the coast of Australia.

Weedy sea dragons grow to be about 18 inches (45 cm) long.

A sea dragon is hard to spot because it has leaf-like growths on its head and body that make it look like seaweed. The sea dragon's color helps it blend in with its surroundings, too.

Leaf Insect

Look closely at this picture. Do you see an insect on the leaf? Leaf insects live in trees in the forests of Asia and Australia. A leaf insect has wide, ribbed wings that fold over its back in the shape of a leaf. It also has growths on its legs that look like leaves. Some leaf insects can also change color to match their surroundings.

The strange shape and color of a leaf insect make it hard to see in the trees. These features help protect the leaf insect from predators. Not many birds looking for food would spot this creature in the trees!

Leaf insects sway back and forth in the wind, just like the leaves they resemble.

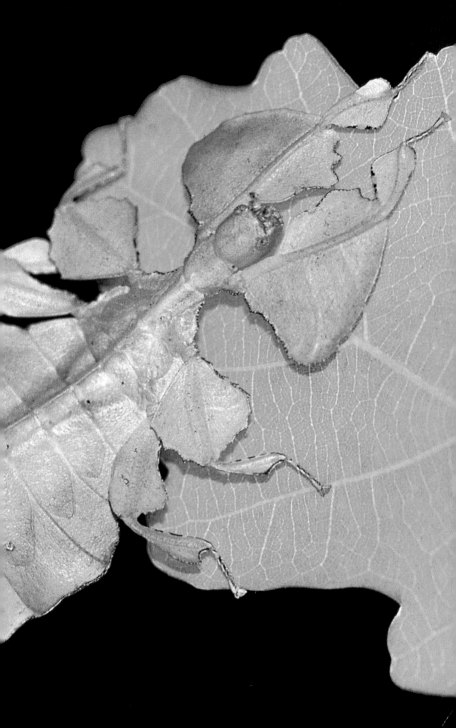

A red-spotted newt has poisonous skin. Touching one won't hurt you, but eating one might make you sick.

Chapter 2

Pretty But Poisonous

Some animals use poison to protect themselves. The European fire salamander can be poisonous to touch, and it can also squirt poison at an attacker. The strength of this poison can kill a small animal. The poison isn't strong enough to kill a human, but it will make a person sick. The salamander's bright colors warn predators to stay away.

European fire salamanders grow to be about six-to-ten inches (15–25 cm) long.

Lionfish live in coral reefs in the warm waters of the Pacific and Indian Oceans.

Lionfish

The lionfish has wide, brightly colored stripes and feathery spikes on its body. These strange features make the lionfish easy to see, but they also mean danger. They are a warning to predators.

A lionfish has poison in its spikes. It can
hurt anything that touches it. Depending on
the species, a lionfish's sting can feel like
a bee sting or it can be fatal. A hungry
predator takes one look at the lionfish and
swims the other way as fast as it can!

Poison Dart Frog

A poison dart frog has pretty, brightly colored skin. A poison dart frog can be yellow, red, orange, green, blue, or black. Their colors help them to survive in the rain forests of Central and South America. Their bright colors tell other animals to stay away!

Only one-to-two inches (3–5 cm) long, the poison dart frog is one of the world's most deadly creatures.

A poison dart frog oozes poison through its skin. The poison can kill other animals. Even licking the skin of this animal can be fatal. When predators see this frog, they leave it alone.

Horned lizards live in desert areas in the western United States and Mexico.

Chapter 3

Super Sprayers

Some animals spray their enemies. They shoot a liquid from their bodies when under attack. The liquid can confuse, surprise, or even poison a predator. The horned lizard can shoot up to one third of its blood at an attacker.

▶ A horned lizard can shoot blood from its eyes.

Octopus

Catching an octopus isn't easy. It is a super sprayer! An octopus can spray a cloud of black ink. The cloud of ink confuses predators. The predators attack the cloud of ink. The octopus then escapes by swimming away quickly.

Most octopuses can change the color of their skin to camouflage themselves.

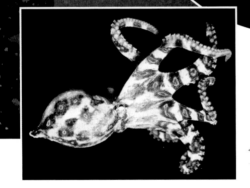

▲ An octopus sprays a cloud of ink when it is provoked.

◀ A blue-ringed octopus has many ways to protect itself.

One type of octopus, the blue-ringed octopus, can also spit deadly poison at its attacker. This animal turns bright yellow with blue rings when it is provoked. The bright colors warn other animals to stay away.

Spitting Cobra

The spitting cobra is a very dangerous snake. This strange animal uses its spitting skills to stop predators. When it is in danger, a spitting cobra sprays venom, or poison, at its attacker. The venom sprays from two small holes near the tip of the snake's fangs, or teeth.

The spitting cobra is a good shot with its spray. It usually hits its attacker in the eyes. The cobra's venom can blind an animal, and

even a person, from up to eight feet away! The venom doesn't hurt if it lands on your skin.

Native to Africa and Asia, different species of spitting cobras can be different colors.

A spitting cobra only sprays venom when it is threatened.

It takes about two days for a crab spider to turn from white to yellow.

Chapter 4

It's a Trick!

Some animals disguise themselves, or pretend to be something else. The crab spider disguises itself to catch its food. It sits on a flower and changes color to match the flower. If a crab spider sits on a white flower, the spider will turn white. If it moves to a yellow flower, the spider will slowly change to yellow. Then it catches any insects that land on the flower. No wonder the insects get caught. They've been tricked.

The crab spider moves sideways like a crab.

Only female anglerfish have glowing spines on their heads.

Anglerfish

An angler is someone who catches fish with a fishing rod. The anglerfish got its name because it has a spine on its head that looks like a fishing rod. This spine has a glowing tip on it that looks like a piece of bait.

The anglerfish lives in the deep ocean where it is very dark. Other fish can't see the anglerfish except for its glowing tip. They see the "bait" and swim toward it. Snap! The anglerfish gobbles its unsuspecting prey.

Stargazer Fish

The stargazer fish is able to trick other fish by making itself look like sand. The stargazer fish buries itself in the sand, with only its eyes, nostrils, and mouth sticking out. Then it waits for other fish to swim by. When one does, the stargazer pops out of the sand and swallows its prey whole.

A stargazer fish hides on the ocean floor and waits for other fish to swim by.

The points on the top of a long-
eared owl's head are feathers,
not ears, and they have nothing
to do with hearing.

Chapter 5

Big Bluffers

Some animals change the shape of their bodies to keep themselves safe. They puff out their bodies or stick out sharp spines and spikes. This makes them look bigger and more difficult to attack. The long-eared owl puffs out its feathers when it is under attack. Then it looks almost twice its size.

A long-eared owl puffs out its feathers when it feels threatened.

Frilled Lizard

The frilled lizard gets its name from the red and orange frill around its neck. The frill usually lies flat against the lizard's body. When the lizard is frightened or under attack, watch out! The lizard opens its mouth very wide. This makes the frill open out like an umbrella. The frill makes the lizard look fierce. Predators, such as hungry birds, are scared away.

The frill around the lizard's neck lays flat when the animal is not frightened.

Frilled lizards
aren't poisonous.
They just look scary.

Porcupinefish

Porcupinefish do not have scales on their skin like most fish. Instead, they have prickly spines. Most of the time, their spines lay against their skin and can't be seen.

When a porcupinefish is in danger, look out! It sucks in lots of water and puffs its body up like a balloon. This makes the fish's prickly spines stick out. Enemies hurry away. No one wants a mouth full of prickly spines!

▶ A porcupinefish can double in size when it puffs out its body.

▼ You can't see the spines on a porcupinefish when it is not feeling threatened.

How to Write an A+ Report

1. Choose a topic.

- Find something that interests you.
- Make sure it is not too big or too small.

2. Find sources.

- Ask your librarian for help.
- Use many different sources: books, magazine articles, and websites.

3. Gather information.

- Take notes. Write down the big ideas and interesting details.
- Use your own words.

4. Organize information.

- Sort your notes into groups that make sense.

- Make an outline. Put your groups of notes in the order you want to write your report.

5. Write your report.

- Write an introduction that tells what the report is about.

- Use your outline and notes as you write to make sure you say everything you want to say in the order you want to say it.

- Write an ending that tells about your report.

- Write a title.

6. Revise and edit your report.

- Read your report to make sure it makes sense.

- Read it again to check spelling, punctuation, and grammar.

7. Hand in your report!

Glossary

bait	something used to attract another animal
camouflage	colors and markings that help animals blend in with their surroundings and hide from enemies
disguise	to change in appearance
fang	a long, pointed tooth
ooze	to leak out slowly
poison	a substance that can harm or kill a living thing
predator	an animal that feeds on other animals
protect	to keep safe
regulate	to adjust
spine	a sharp, pointed object that sticks out from an animal's body
venom	a poison made by snakes and other animals to harm their attackers

Further Reading

• Books •

Animal Encyclopedia. New York, NY: DK Children, 2000. Ages 9-12, 376 pages.

Kalman, Bobbie. *What Are Camouflage and Mimicry?* New York, NY: Crabtree Publishing Company, 2001. Ages 9-12, 32 pages.

Lovett, Sarah. *Animal Disguises (Extremely Weird).* Emeryville, CA: Avalon Travel Publishing, 1997. Ages 9-12, 30 pages.

Lovett, Sarah. *Insects (Extremely Weird).* Emeryville, CA: Avalon Travel Publishing, 1996. Ages 9-12, 30 pages.

Lovett, Sarah. *Reptiles (Extremely Weird).* Emeryville, CA: Avalon Travel Publishing, 1996. Ages 9-12, 30 pages.

National Geographic Animal Encyclopedia. Washington, DC: National Geographic Society, 2000. Ages 8-12, 264 pages.

Parsons, Alexandria. *Amazing Poisonous Animals (Eyewitness Junior).* New York, NY: Knopf Books for Young Readers, 1990. Ages 9-12, 30 pages.

Pringle, Laurence. *Scholastic Encyclopedia of Animals.* New York, NY: Scholastic, 2001. Ages 8-12, 128 pages.

• Websites •

Australian Museum Online
http://www.amonline.net.au/

Desert USA
http://desertusa.com/index.html

Enchanted Learning
http://www.enchantedlearning.com/Home.html

KidCyber
http://www.kidcyber.com.au/topics/animals.htm

San Diego Zoo
http://www.sandiegozoo.org/

Wikipedia Online Encyclopedia
http://en.wikipedia.org/wiki/Main_Page

World Almanac for Kids Online
http://www.worldalmanacforkids.com/index.html

Index

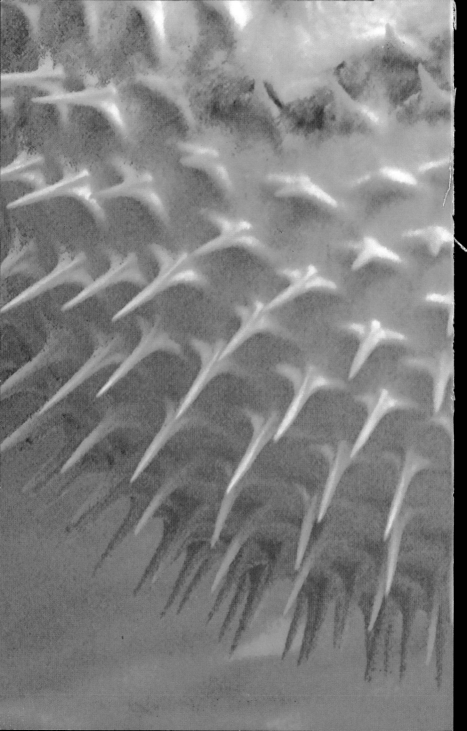